Woodcarving a *Christmas* Chess Set

Photo credits:

Dwayne Gosnell: 7, 48, and all step-by-step photos

Mike Mihalo: front and back cover, 2-3, 4-5, 6, 8, 9, 16–17, 18, and all photos of finished chess pieces

Courtesy Shutterstock: Sandra Cunningham 16–17 (Christmas tree background); Fortyforks, 17 (top right); primopiano cover, 1, 2, 4-5, 17 (wood background); Verock 19, 23, 26, 30, 34, 39

ISBN 978-1-4971-0137-1

Library of Congress Control Number: 2020014041

To learn more about the other great books from Fox Chapel Publishing, or to find a retailer near you, call toll-free 800-457-9112 or visit us at *www.FoxChapelPublishing.com*.

We are always looking for talented authors. To submit an idea, please send a brief inquiry to acquisitions@foxchapelpublishing.com.

Printed in China
First printing

WOODCARVING A *Christmas* CHESS SET

PATTERNS AND INSTRUCTIONS FOR
Caricature Carving

Dwayne Gosnell

Fox Chapel
PUBLISHING

Contents

Acknowledgments

I want to extend my deepest thanks to everyone along the way who told me to keep carving and never give up.

Dedication

To my loving wife, Melissa, for always supporting me throughout the endless woodchips, and to my daughter and son for always being there to help make the funny funnier.

Before You Carve

Basic Carving Instructions

All you really need in order to carve is a space to complete your project, a comfy chair, some wood, and the carving tools of your choice. I've never met a carver who wasn't also a tool collector. If you have it, use it. If I use a certain tool in the instructions, but you can accomplish the same thing with a different tool, do it. Here are some points to remember:

- Make sure that your tools are as sharp as they can be. You shouldn't force dull tools into the wood.
- Carve as much as you can every day. Don't be afraid to challenge yourself.
- Don't carve while tired, as this can lead to miscuts—either in the wood or your hand.
- Always use protective gear, such as gloves and finger guards.
- Remember that everyone makes mistakes—it's only a block of wood! Don't expect to create a perfect carving right away; the fun is in the journey.

Getting Started

Just like in chess, you need to plan and think ahead when carving a chess set. Luckily, I have taken some of the planning out of it by providing a list to get you started (see page 8). All of the pieces are cut from 2" (5.1cm) square basswood stock. You will need a bandsaw or access to one due to the number of carvings. You can cut the pieces out with a coping saw, but with thirty-two pieces per chess set, it could take a while.

For expediency, I cut out all of the pieces in the set prior to carving.

Always protect your hands while carving. To keep your knife blade sharp, apply stropping compound to a piece of leather. Then, with the bevel facing away from you, pull the knife toward you across the stropping compound in a reverse shaving-type motion—you don't want the blade to dig into the leather.

Cutting Out the Blanks

1 Place the front and side patterns on the basswood blank. You can draw around the pattern (like I have done), attach the pattern with repositionable spray adhesive, or use graphite paper and a pencil to transfer the pattern onto the wood.

2 Cut the front view. Tape the waste wood back in place; this will provide stability and a reference point when cutting the adjacent view.

3 Cut the adjacent side.

4 Remove the blank from the waste wood. *Note: Take your time! Speed is not your friend in these steps. I used a ¼" (6mm)–wide blade with six TPI (teeth per inch); however, you could use a smaller blade if desired.*

Materials and Tools

MATERIALS:

- Basswood, 2" (5.1cm) square (quantities given are for one complete chess set):
  - Pawns: 16 blocks at 3¾" (9.5cm) tall
  - Rooks: 4 blocks at 4" (10cm) tall
  - Knights: 4 blocks at 4⅜" (11cm) tall
  - Bishops: 4 blocks at 4¾" (12cm) tall
  - Queens: 2 blocks at 5" (13cm) tall
  - Kings: 2 blocks at 5½" (14cm) tall
- Patterns and graphite paper, stylus, or pencil
- Carving glove: Your choice, but make sure that your carving glove fits snug to your hand. A loose carving glove will allow the tool to grab and possibly slice into your hand or fingers.

TOOLS:

I used the following tools to create the chess set. Feel free to use the tools you have available or what works best for you.

- Bandsaw (I use a ¼" [6mm] blade with six TPI [teeth per inch])
- Carving knife of choice
- Detail knife of choice
- Hole punch (eye punch), ¼" (6mm)
- 45° V-tool, ⅛" (3mm)
- 45° V-tool, ¼" (6mm)
- 90° V-tool, ½" (13mm)
- V-tool, soft, ⅜" (10mm)
- #7 gouge, ¾" (19mm)
- #9 gouge, ⅛" (3mm)
- #9 gouge, ¼" (6mm)

PAINT:

A paint chart is provided on page 17, with individual paint colors listed after each project.

PAINTBRUSHES:

I don't get picky about sizes, but make sure that you have quality brushes.

V-Tool Layers

Lay the V-tool on its side to create layers in wood easily. This helps separate clothing and prevents the need to make a lot of knife stops and relief cuts on your project. It also saves time; instead of having to make and carve up to a bunch of stop cuts, you can relieve certain areas in just one pass.

Practice

Carving Eyes

Carving the eyes is easily the most stressful challenge to a carver of any skill level. After all, the eyes are the first thing that everyone sees when looking at a carving. However, with this easy approach, I hope to show you that carving eyes is nothing to be afraid of and can even be quite simple.

Practice carving eyes on a separate block of scrap wood prior to carving the project.

1 Start in the center of the upper eyelid, cutting toward the nose, with a ¼" (6mm) 45° V-tool. Then, with the same V-tool, complete the other half of the upper eyelid. If you find this V-tool too large, use a ⅛" (3mm) 45° V-tool instead.

2 With the V-tool you used in step 1, cut the lower part of the upper eyelid, which will be the eye opening. Then cut the lower eyelid to complete the eye opening.

3 With your favorite knife (I use a detail knife for eyes), carve a triangle-shaped chip on each side of the eyeball and then remove the chip cleanly. The lowest point of the chip should be closest to the edge of the eye, making the eyeball appear round.

4 Define the eyelids with the knife you used in step 3. This will create shadows, which add depth and interest to the eye area.

5 Using the same knife, spend a bit of time making the eyes round. The rounder the eye, the better it looks. Thin the upper eyelids. Make sure there are no hidden or hanging chips.

Steps 1–5

Carving Noses

The nose of any piece can set the tone for how the entire face will look. Will the nose be too small, too big, too thin, too flat? Calm down, my friend! Your nose will look great as long as you plan out what you want and stick to the plan. I start each nose by planning to carve it a bit bigger than needed—remember, we can't add wood back once it's gone.

Note: Think in flat planes for a simple approach, and use the tool that fits the carving; no sizes are exact.

1 Cut into the blank, carving upward from the tip of the nose with your carving knife (which you will use for all of these steps unless otherwise indicated). Then carve down to the deepest point of the first cut from the opposite side, creating a low area (valley). Remove the chip you just created.

2 Cut upward along the top right side of the valley and remove the chip as you did in step 1.

3 Cut upward along the top left side of the valley and remove the chip as you did in step 1.

4 Cut downward along the bottom of the tip of the nose. Remove the chip by cutting upward from the chin area.

5 On one side of the nose, cut downward and then remove the chip as you did in step 4.

6 On the other side of the nose, cut downward and then remove the chip as you did in step 4.

7 With a V-tool, carve the sides of the nose. Notice that the side of the tool closest to the nose follows the same angle as the nose. Do not cut straight into the nose.

8 With the knife, remove a triangle in the corner of the nose. This will round the bottom slightly.

9 Repeat the process in step 8 on the opposite side.

10 Deepen the bridge of the nose to create more of a profile.

11 With a gouge, remove the wood above the nostrils by carving upward to the eye area.

12 With the same tool, carve from the outside of the face inward, removing the chip. This creates the eye socket as well.

13 With the knife, carve shadow lines around the nostril. Again, do not undercut or cut straight into the nose.

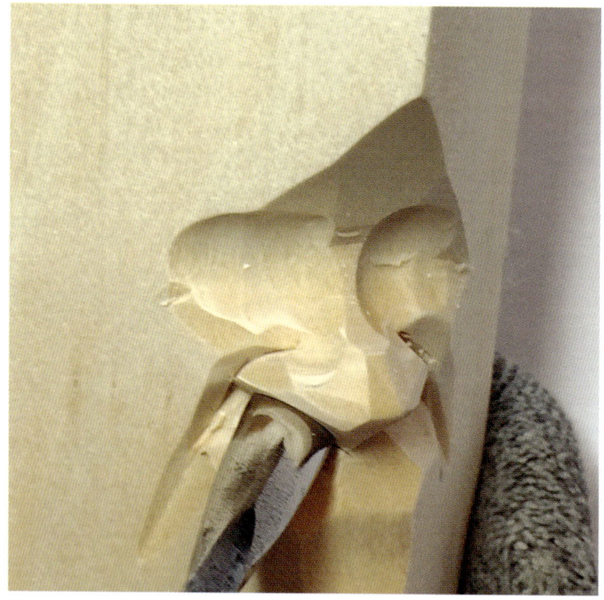

14 Establish the nostrils. Using a small gouge turned upside down, push straight into the wood, not upward. You can pop the chip out by taking the tip of your knife and carefully pushing the chip downward. It will break the chip, but that's OK.

15 With the knife, cut inward in the first step of a triangle.

16 Make the second cut of the triangle.

17 Remove the chip, finishing the triangle. The deepest point should be right in the center of the chip.

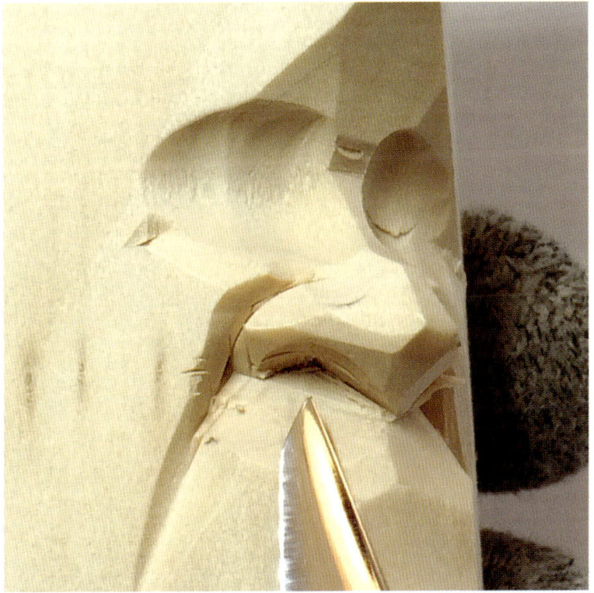

18 Progress! Make careful cuts to remove the "fuzzies." Notice that the triangle makes the opening look deeper. From this point, you could make the nose longer by removing more wood from the bridge of the nose if desired.

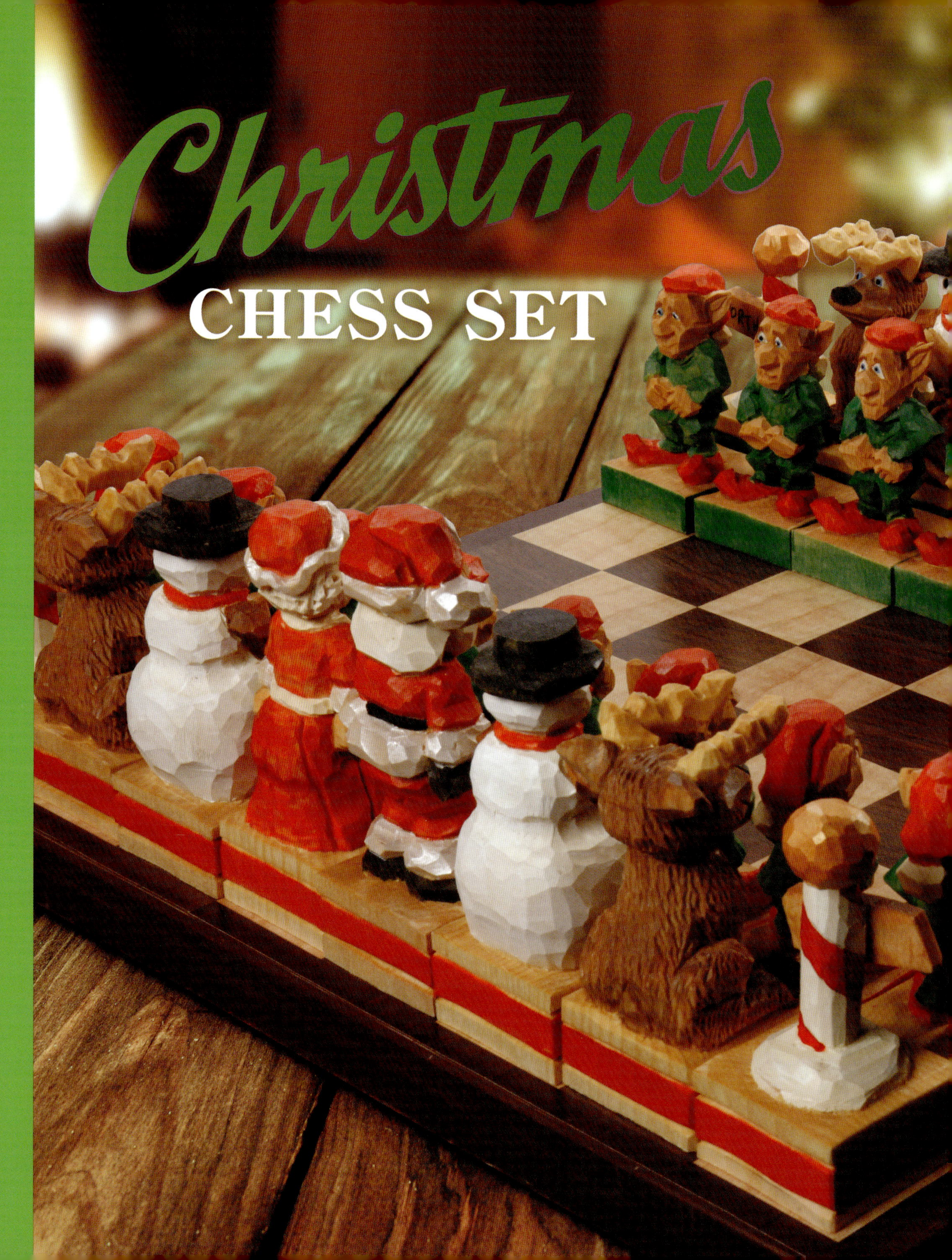

Christmas
CHESS SET

Christmas is a universal season with rich traditions. For my family, it is a time to show our love and gratitude for each other—a time when, no matter the weather outside, we still find that the Christmas spirit warms our hearts. As a child, I could never imagine anyone loving Christmas as much as I did, until I became a father and saw my children on Christmas Day. Growing up as an only child, I never had to compete with anyone to get the best gift. As a father of two, I watch my kids plan and battle it out like a friendly game of chess for months as they try to climb to the top of Santa's "nice list."

The hardest thing is explaining to my kids why there are so many different Santas in the various stores we visit in December. While I have a looming fear that the kids are "figuring it out," I simply explain that the Santas are magical. But, in my adult mind, I think, *What if the Santas had to fight for the title of Mr. Claus?* And the chess set idea was born.

Paint Colors

The author used these products for the projects. Substitute your choices of brands and colors as desired.

Apple Barrel
- Antique Parchment (matte)
- Black (matte)
- Blue Bonnet (matte)
- Bright Red (matte)
- Brown Oxide (matte)
- Christmas Green (matte)
- Nutmeg Brown (matte)
- Pumpkin Orange (matte)
- White (matte)

DecoArt
- Cotton Ball (satin)
- White Pearl (metallic)

Jo Sonja
- Rich Gold (matte)

Minwax
- Honeycomb (water-based stain)

Christmas Pawn

There are more pawns in a chess set than any other piece, and the pawns usually do most of the work. The same can be said about the elves in Santa's North Pole workshop and all of the responsibility they have.

In carving the pawns (elves), I found that the vast amount of them (sixteen in the set) can be a bit much to carve all at once. I suggest carving two pawns and then carving another piece in the set to break up the project. If you are the type of person who doesn't like to skip around, I suggest carving the pawns first to get the hard part out of the way.

1 With the pattern cut out, draw in the head, arms, legs, and centerline of the face. With the ⅜" (10mm) soft V-tool, block out these areas and narrow the sides of the face toward the nose.

2 With the same tool, define the chest area, separating it from the top of the hands.

3 With your carving knife, carve the nose as described in Carving Noses, starting on page 11. Carve the forearms from the wrist area back to the elbow area.

4 With the ¼" (6mm) 45° V-tool, carve the arms and the smile lines on the face, and separate the hat from the forehead.

5 With the same tool, separate the legs in back. With the carving knife, establish the hat ball and separate the backs of the arms from the torso.

6 With the ½" (13mm) 90° V-tool, narrow the face. This cut also creates the front of what will be the sideburns.

7 With the carving knife, further shape the arms and remove all remaining saw marks. Then use the knife to separate the legs and shoes at the same time. Be careful not to twist the knife in these areas, as this can snap off the tip.

8 With the ⅛" (3mm) 45° V-tool, carve all of the clothing lines and the eyes (see page 10), mouth, and sideburns.

9 With the same tool, carve the hands (fingers) and the details of the inner ears. With the carving knife, clean up all hidden chips and hanging pieces and then clean up the base, creating a level, clean plane for the shoes to stand on.

Pawn Paint Key

Front

- Brown Oxide 50/50
- Black 100%
- White 100%
- Blue Bonnet 100%
- Honeycomb 50/50
- Christmas Green 50/50
- Bright Red 50/50
- Antique Parchment 50/50 (ball of hat)
- Bright Red 50/50 or Christmas Green 50/50*

100% = full-strength
50/50 = 50% paint 50% water, mixed
* Side 1 bases = Bright Red 50/50
  Side 2 bases = Christmas Green 50/50

Side

Back

Christmas Rook

When designing the rook, I found myself thinking about where castles were located. This time, I took the concept of location very literally and made the North Pole sign.

The rook is a simple carving and can give you a sense of completion when finished. I suggest carving the rooks as a reward, so to speak, after finishing the pawns.

1 With the pattern cut out, remove the wood from the back of what will be the sign with the knife. Shape the pole from a square to a rough octagon shape with the carving knife. Remove all of the saw marks from the piece.

2 With your carving knife, shape what will be the ball at the top of the pole from square to octagon. Make short, controlled cuts to shape the top of the post, stopping each cut as the piece changes direction.

3 Refine the shape of the pole and the ball at the top with the carving knife. Shape the snow at the base of the sign to make it round.

4 Clean up the base with the carving knife.

5 With the ¼" (6mm) 45° V-tool, carve two lines around the base to add a bit of interest.

NORTH POLE

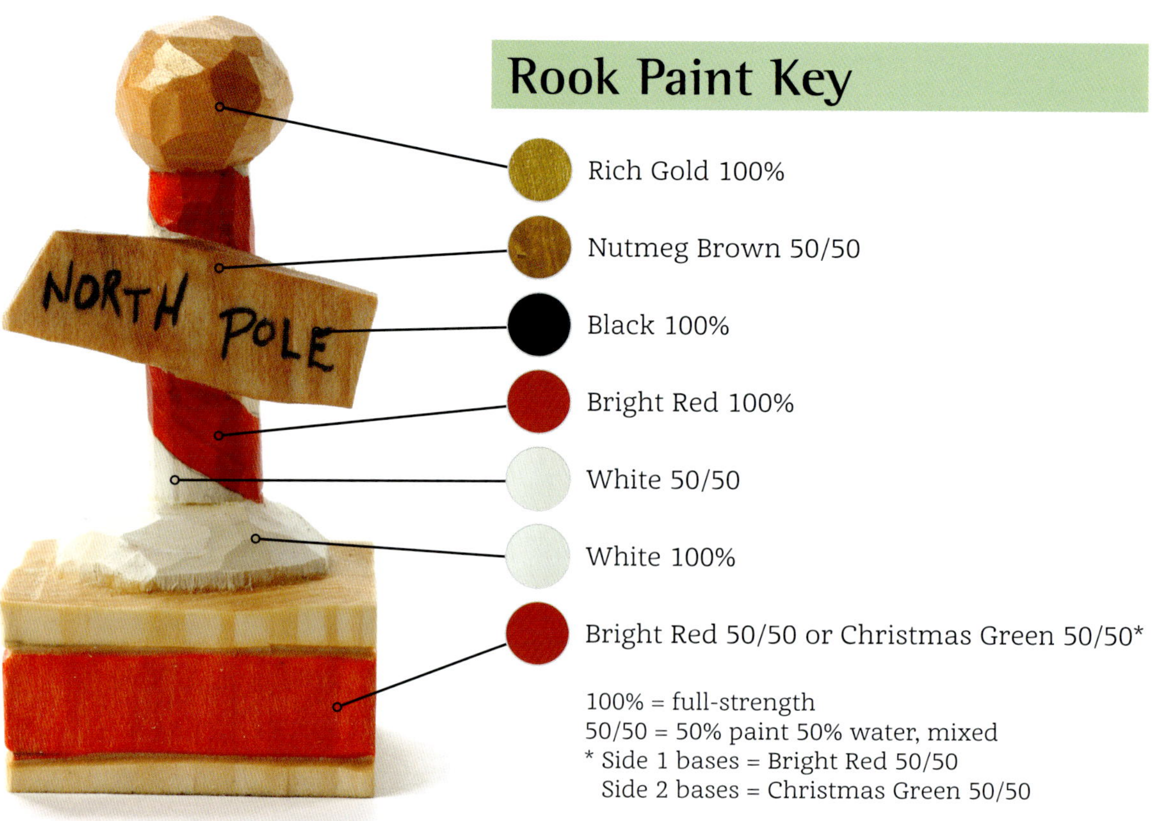

Rook Paint Key

Rich Gold 100%

Nutmeg Brown 50/50

Black 100%

Bright Red 100%

White 50/50

White 100%

Bright Red 50/50 or Christmas Green 50/50*

100% = full-strength
50/50 = 50% paint 50% water, mixed
* Side 1 bases = Bright Red 50/50
   Side 2 bases = Christmas Green 50/50

Front

Side

Back

Christmas Knight

I found humor in representing the knight pieces with reindeer in this Christmas set.

The knight is simple but complex: it's simple in that only a few tools are needed, but it's complex when you realize that the reindeer is covered in fur. Break the carving down into steps and treat the hair as the last step. You will have these knights flying off your carving bench in no time.

1 With the pattern cut out, mark the legs, head, tail, ears, and antlers. I used a ⅜" (10mm) soft V-tool to block out these areas because I like the softer cuts that the soft V-tool creates in the low areas.

2 On the top of the piece, establish where the antlers will sit. Note that they create a V pattern. Remove the bulk of the wood with the same soft V-tool.

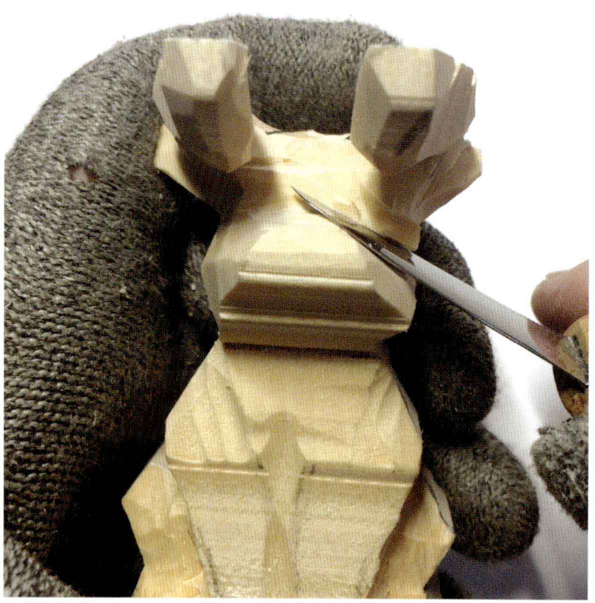

3 With your favorite carving knife, shape the snout area by carving along the sides and then curving the blade upward to create the eye area.

4 With the carving knife, carve off all of the "corners," rounding the body parts.

5 With the ⅛" (3mm) 45° V-tool, carve the eyes (see page 10), the nose (see page 11), mouth, ears, and hooves. Give him a big, round nose and a wide smile.

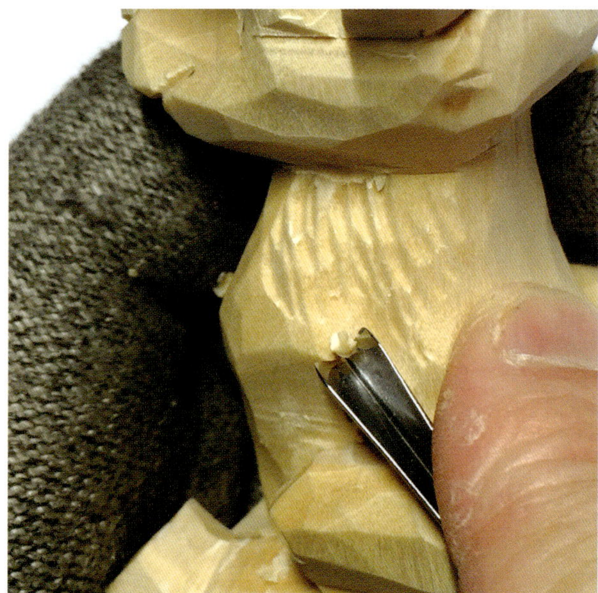

6 With the ¼" (6mm) #9 gouge, refine the grooves in the antlers. Be careful, as the smaller you make the antlers, the more likely they are to break. I tend to leave mine on the fatter side. After you have achieved a good separation, carve the tips to a point with the carving knife.

7 With ¼" (6mm) 45° V-tool, carve the fur texture. This is time consuming but well worth it. Pay attention to the way that the fur will lay on the piece. Do not draw in the fur, as your carving will get messy quickly. Make short cuts, around ¹⁄₁₆" (2mm) to ⅛" (3mm) long, with the ¼" (6mm) 45° V-tool. With the fur texture carved, take the time to get rid of any hanging chips with the carving knife.

8 With the ¼" (6mm) 45° V-tool, carve two lines around the base to add a bit of interest. Clean up all hidden chips with the knife.

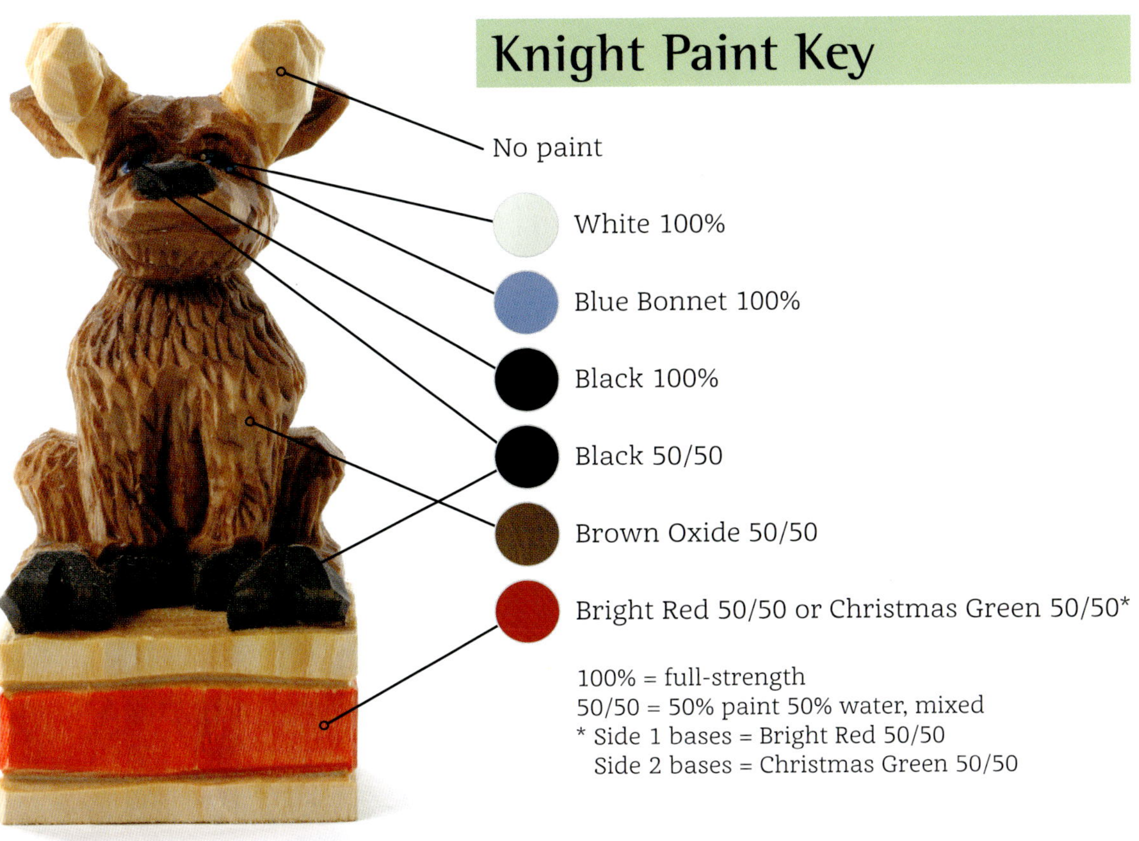

No paint

White 100%

Blue Bonnet 100%

Black 100%

Black 50/50

Brown Oxide 50/50

Bright Red 50/50 or Christmas Green 50/50*

100% = full-strength
50/50 = 50% paint 50% water, mixed
* Side 1 bases = Bright Red 50/50
  Side 2 bases = Christmas Green 50/50

Front

Side

Back

Christmas Bishop

I think of the bishop as a wise recordkeeper—so casting a meltable snowman as the one in charge of records seemed fitting in an ironic way.

When carving the bishop, don't worry too much about making him perfect. After all, he has a carrot nose and tree-branch arms and was possibly made by children. Have fun, make clean cuts, and watch him come to life!

1 With the pattern cut out, establish where the arms and scroll will be. Remove the corners from the entire piece with the carving knife—don't forget the hat.

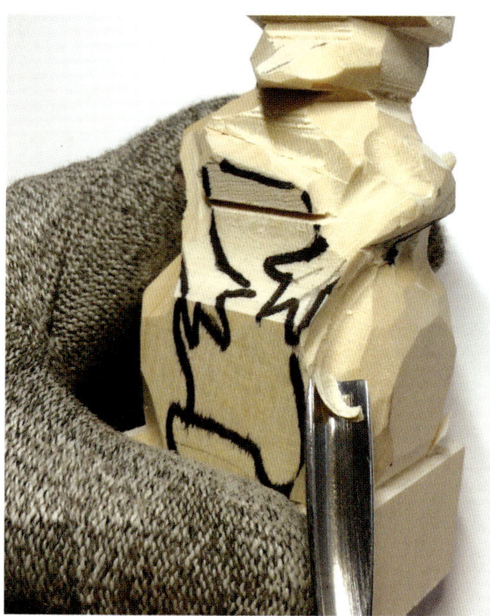

2 With the ⅜" (10mm) soft V-tool, separate the arms from the body and the sides of the scroll. Leave a bit of wood above the scroll on the right side as you look at it. This will become part of the scarf later.

3 With the ¼" (6mm) 45° V-tool, carve the hands. Remember, the arms and hands are made from sticks, so make branch-like fingers.

4 With the carving knife, remove any pencil or pen marks.

5 With the carving knife, carve the hand details a bit deeper, cleaning up the V-tool marks. Then clean up the arms with the knife, giving them a twiggy shape.

6 With a large gouge, round the stacked snowball torso, separating the snowball shapes that comprise the snowman's body.

7 Refine the torso with the carving knife. Don't worry about getting it super-smooth; you want it to look carved.

8 With the ¼" (6mm) 45° V-tool, carve a scarf around the neck area. With the wood that you left in step 2, carve the knot and the scarf ends hanging down. Carve the mouth with same tool.

9 With your hole punch (eye punch), make the round eyes. They don't have to be perfectly level—he's a snowman!

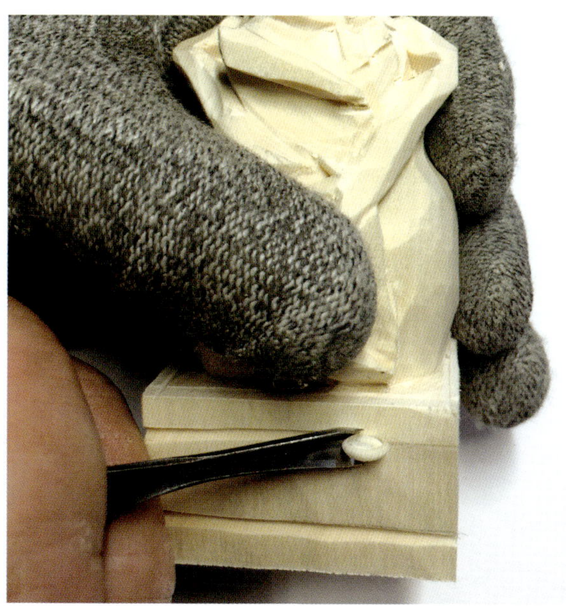

10 With the ¼" (6mm) 45° V-tool, carve two lines around the base to add a bit of interest. Clean up all hanging chips with the carving knife.

Bishop Paint Key

- Black 50/50
- Black 100%
- Pumpkin Orange 50/50
- Bright Red 50/50
- Nutmeg Brown 50/50
- Cotton Ball 100%
- No paint
- Bright Red 50/50 or Christmas Green 50/50*

100% = full-strength
50/50 = 50% paint 50% water, mixed
* Side 1 bases = Bright Red 50/50
  Side 2 bases = Christmas Green 50/50

Front

Side

Back

Christmas King

The king of any empire is usually the most recognized figure around. It was an easy choice to make Santa the king of this chess set. Let's face it: Santa only works once a year, after everyone else is tired. The same can be said in chess: the king only moves when he absolutely has to.

The king is a straightforward carving, and you need only a few tools. Carve nice, clean lines where color transitions will happen. This will reduce the likelihood of paint colors bleeding into each other later.

1 With the pattern cut out, establish where the arms and hat will be. Remove the areas at the front and back of the arms with the ⅜" (10mm) soft V-tool from the torso. Also remove the wood around the hat, relieving the top of the hat as it hangs.

2 With the same tool, remove all of the saw marks from the valleys in the carving.

3 With your favorite carving knife, shape the face so it tapers slightly toward the nose. Remove all of the sharp corners from the rest of the carving. Set the bridge of the nose.

4 With the ¼" (6mm) 45° V-tool, carve all of the separation lines: the legs, shoes, arms, clothing, hat, and anywhere else a separation point exists within the piece.

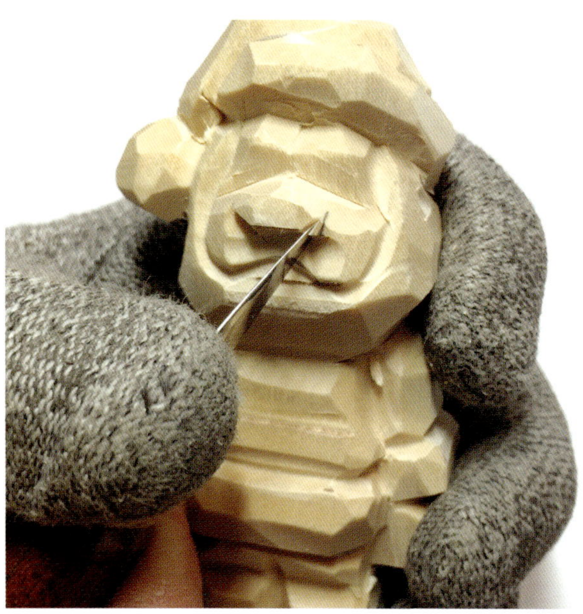

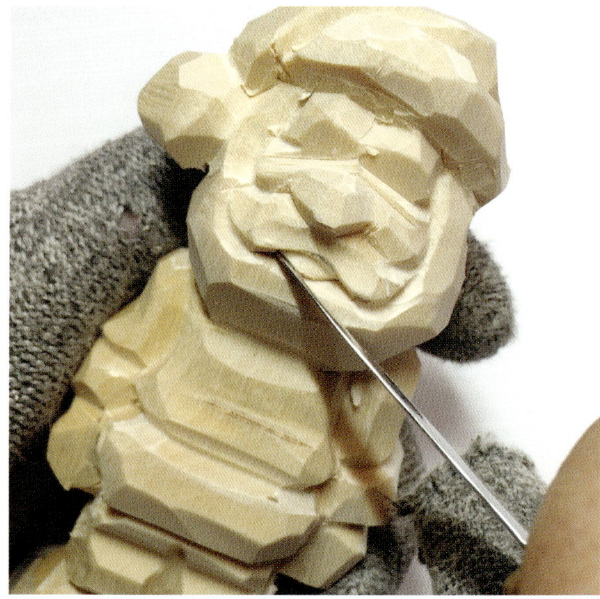

5 Carve the nose as indicated in the Carving Noses section, beginning on page 11.

6 With the carving knife, shape the mouth. Think of two triangles on the bottom of either side, creating a round bottom lip.

7 With the carving knife, carve a bit deeper between the legs and arms, creating shadow lines. Do not carve all the way through the legs on this piece.

8 With the carving knife, go around the entire piece to create more shadows: carve a small triangular chip wherever there is a separation between clothing and stopping points.

9 With the carving knife, separate the hair from the beard.

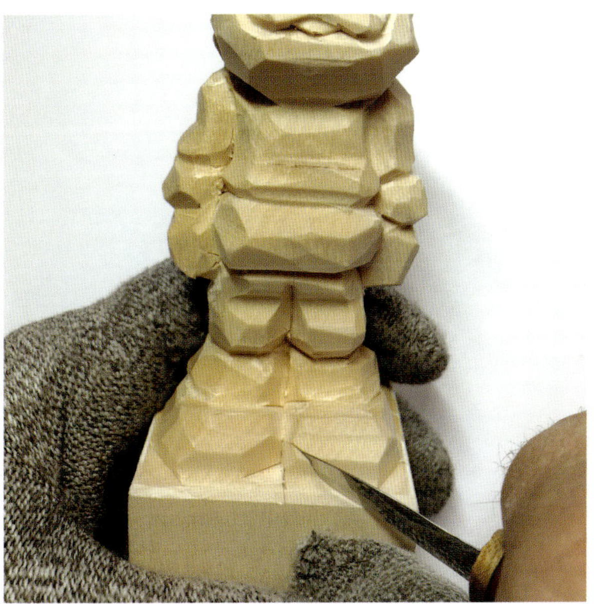

10 With the same knife, shape the shoes. I tend to block the shoes in instead of attempting to carve them super-round. This makes the piece look carved and hold shadow lines during painting.

11 With the ¼" (6mm) 45° V-tool, carve the thumb by removing some width of the wood from the hand. Be careful carving downward, as you are carving with the grain, and too much pressure can cause the wood to split. Finish the thumb by curving the bottom toward the body.

12 With the ⅛" (3mm) 45° V-tool, carve the eyes and upper eyelids (see page 10.)

13 With the ¼" (6mm) 45° V-tool, carve two lines around the base to add a bit of interest. Clean up all hanging chips with the carving knife.

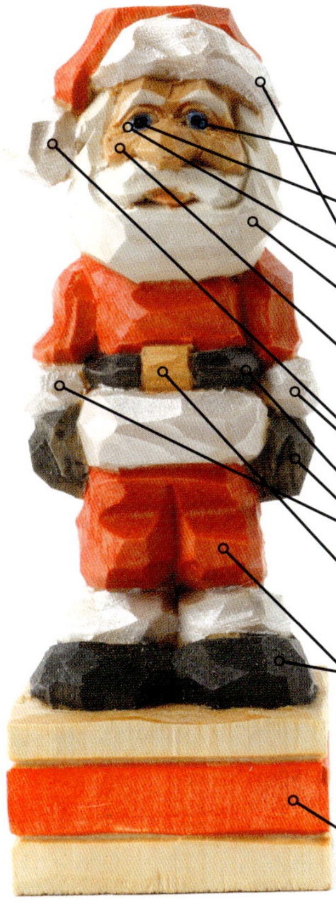

King Paint Key

- Blue Bonnet 100%
- Black 100%
- White 100%
- White 50/50
- Honeycomb 50/50
- White Pearl 100%
- Black 50/50
- Rich Gold 100%
- Bright Red 50/50
- Bright Red 50/50 or Christmas Green 50/50*

100% = full-strength
50/50 = 50% paint 50% water, mixed
* Side 1 bases = Bright Red 50/50
  Side 2 bases = Christmas Green 50/50

Front

Side

Back

Christmas Queen

CHRISTMAS CHESS SET

In chess—as is often the case in life—the queen is the toughest character in the room. Naturally, my queen is Mrs. Claus. She is the voice of reason, keeping Santa on track and focused.

In carving Mrs. Claus, I find that I need to slow down and make smaller, softer cuts around the face. I carve Mrs. Claus last, finishing with the most powerful piece.

1 With the pattern cut out, draw in the reference lines. With the ⅜" (10mm) soft V-tool, separate the arms from the torso and narrow the face on the sides so it fits under the bonnet.

2 With the same tool, separate the hair from the bonnet and separate the dress ruffles and hands.

3 With your favorite carving knife, remove all of the sharp corners from the entire piece, rounding the carving.

4 With the same knife, shape the face from the centerline back toward the hairline.

5 With the same tool, establish the top and bottom of the nose. This is just for reference.

6 With a shallow gouge of your choice, remove the saw marks from the low areas and continue to round the torso.

7 With a ¼" (6mm) 45° V-tool, separate the exposed shoe from the dress and carve the dress ruffles on the arms.

8 With the carving knife, refine the dress details and hands. Remove any remaining saw marks from the piece, again rounding the torso.

9 With the ¼" (6mm) 45° V-tool, carve the top of the ruffle on the bonnet. This will sit about ¼" (6mm) above the original bonnet line all the way around.

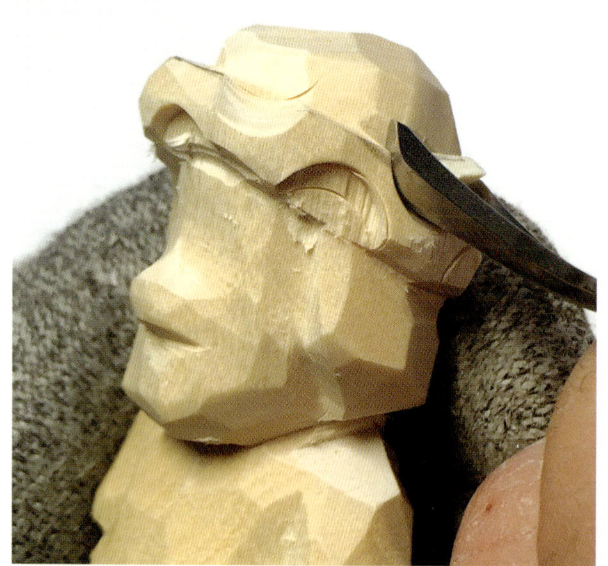

10 With a gouge (I used a ⅜" [10mm] #9), carve above and below the ruffle line, alternating to create movement in the bonnet.

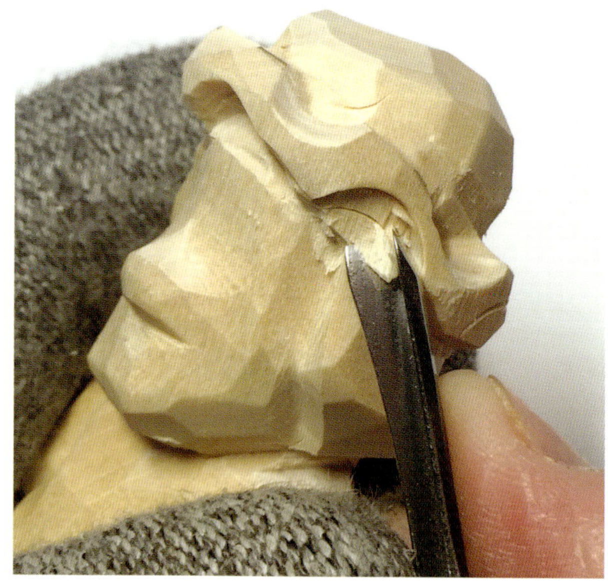

11 With the ¼" (6mm) 45° V-tool, clean up the ruffles.

12 With the ¼" (6mm) 45° V-tool, carve the apron and apron strings. Pay attention to the layers; remember that laying the V-tool on its side creates easy layering in clothes. Carve the apron string in the back, wrapping it around the waist.

13 With the carving knife, clean up the corners of the carving.

14 With the ⅜" (10mm) #9 gouge, carve the eye sockets (see page 10) and separate the eyebrows. With the ⅛" (3mm) 45° V-tool, carve the eyes, mouth, and smile lines. Finish carving the nose (see page 11).

15 With the ¼" (6mm) 45° V-tool, carve triangles to create a curly texture for the hair.

16 With the ¼" (6mm) 45° V-tool, carve vertical lines in the bottom of the dress to create the look and texture of an old-fashioned hoop skirt.

17 With the ¼" (6mm) 45° V-tool, carve two lines around the base to add a bit of interest. Clean up all hidden chips with the carving knife.

Queen Paint Key

- White 100%
- White 50/50
- Blue Bonnet 100%
- Black 100%
- White Pearl 100%
- Bright Red 50/50
- Honeycomb 50/50
- Antique Parchment 50/50
- Black 50/50
- Bright Red 50/50 or Christmas Green 50/50*

100% = full-strength
50/50 = 50% paint 50% water, mixed
* Side 1 bases = Bright Red 50/50
  Side 2 bases = Christmas Green 50/50

Patterns

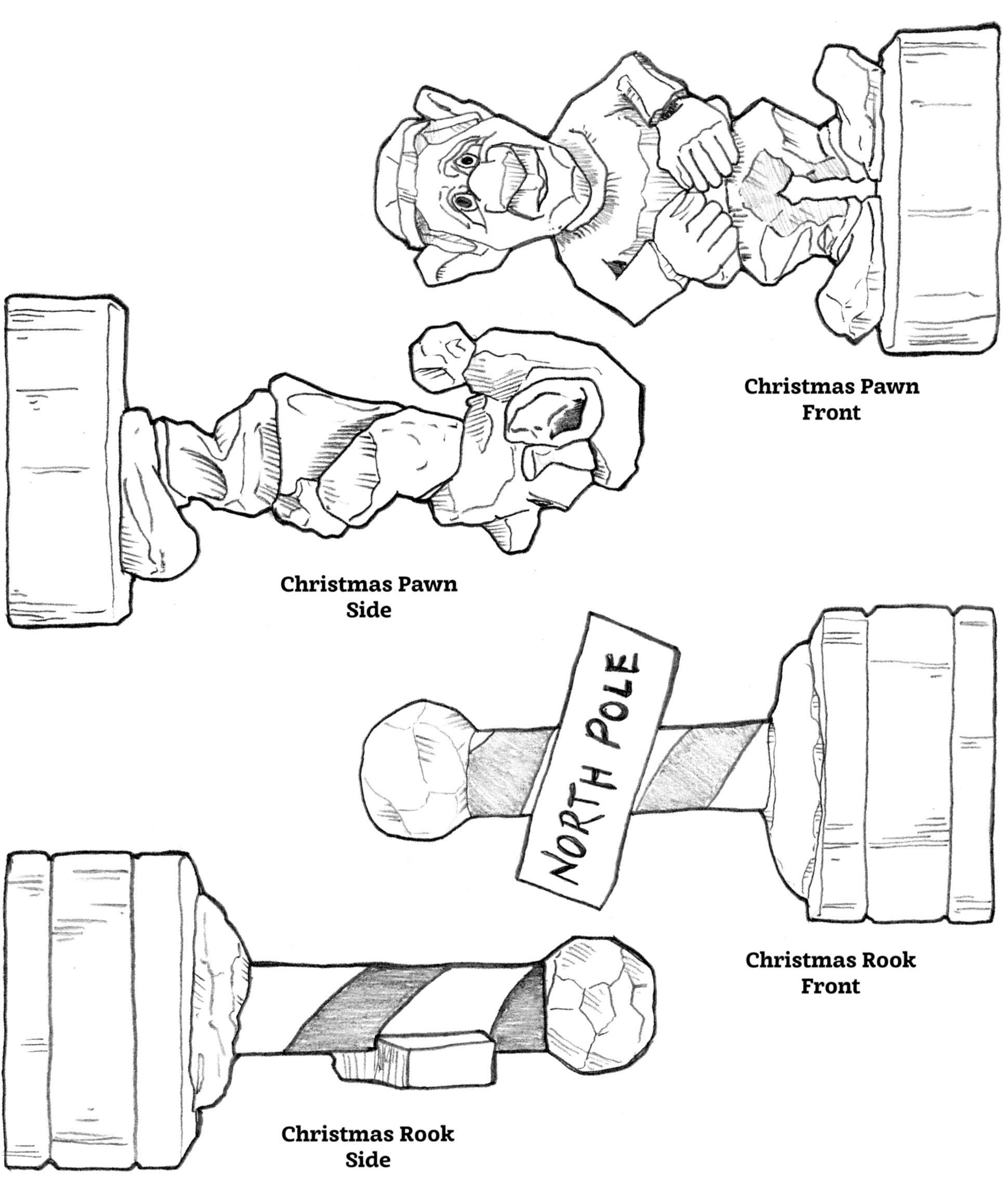

**Christmas Pawn
Front**

**Christmas Pawn
Side**

**Christmas Rook
Front**

**Christmas Rook
Side**

**Christmas Knight
Front**

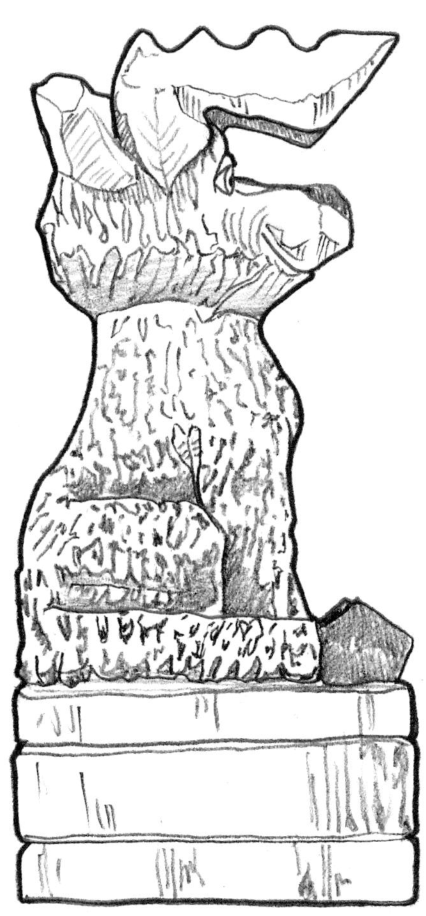

**Christmas Knight
Side**

**Christmas Bishop
Front**

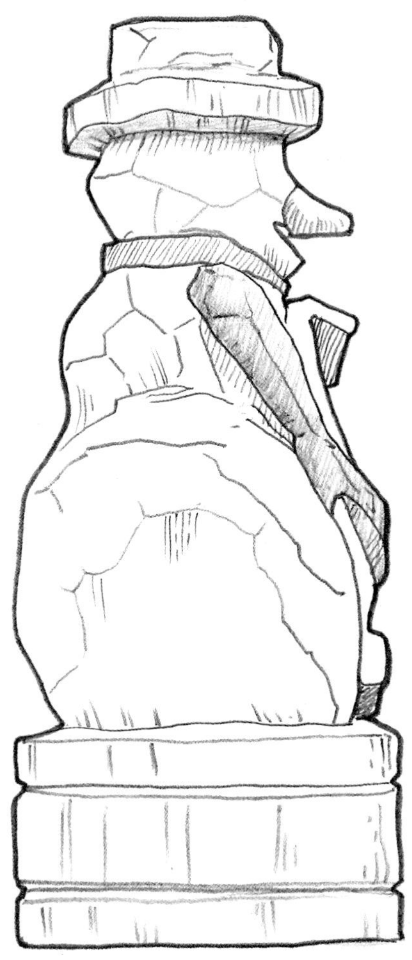

**Christmas Bishop
Side**

**Christmas King
Front**

**Christmas King
Side**

**Christmas Queen
Front**

**Christmas Queen
Side**

About the Author

DWAYNE GOSNELL grew up in a small town in North Carolina, dreaming of the day when he would go off into the world and make his mark. In his childhood, he would often help his father with woodworking projects, and he enjoyed the process of creating something from nothing. It wasn't until later in life, after serving in the Marine Corps, that he was thrown back into creating. He happened into a local woodworking shop and purchased a book about carving faces into walking sticks. After two visits to the emergency room, dozens of boxes of bandages, and countless trips back to the woodworking shop for more books, the man behind the counter said with a grin, "You know we have a carving club, right?" The man gave Dwayne information about the Catawba Valley Woodcarvers and told him to bring some carvings for "show and tell."

At Dwayne's first meeting, he walked into the crowded stockroom carrying a bag filled with two tools, some carving books, and a dozen tree limbs with butchered faces carved into them. He sat alone in the back and thought, *There's no way I'm opening this bag of junk in front of these master carvers.* With the life-sized birds and amazing caricatures the others had brought, Dwayne was overwhelmed.

When he heard a female voice say "hi," he looked and saw Paige Cartledge. Little did he know that it would start a conversation that fueled his fire for caricature carving. Paige's husband, Mitch, agreed to teach Dwayne a thing or two...or a lot. Dwayne carved with Mitch on Monday nights for almost a year, and he became addicted to everything caricature. Even though he wasn't good at it yet, he had an amazing teacher and was determined to absorb everything about caricature carving.

Fast-forward more than a decade, and now Dwayne is the guy who's sharing what he's learned and how to avoid the mistakes he's made. He is president of the Catawba Valley Woodcarvers and teaches classes around the United States. He owns rough-out patterns for the Phil and Vicki Bishop Collection as well as most of Steve Brown's rough-out collection. In February 2020, he was inducted into the Caricature Carvers of America.

Dwayne lives in Hickory, North Carolina, with his wife, Melissa, and his two children, Payton and Mason. He works in law enforcement, and carving has always been a way for him to unwind after a long day. Throughout the years, what started as a hobby has become an endless passion to create. He has won many awards, but the friendships he has made are worth far more than any of them.

For more information, visit Dwayne's website, *dgosnellwoodcarving.com*.